A Guide to
AMERICAN STATES

New Mexico

THE LAND OF ENCHANTMENT

MEDIA ENHANCED BOOKS
AV2
BY WEIGL
ADDED VALUE • AUDIO VISUAL

www.av2books.com

AV² provides enriched content that supplements and complements this book. Weigl's AV² books strive to create inspired learning and engage young minds in a total learning experience.

Your AV² Media Enhanced books come alive with...

Audio
Listen to sections of the book read aloud.

Key Words
Study vocabulary, and complete a matching word activity.

Video
Watch informative video clips.

Quizzes
Test your knowledge.

Go to **www.av2books.com**, and enter this book's unique code.

BOOK CODE

V 4 3 0 5 5 6

Embedded Weblinks
Gain additional information for research.

Slide Show
View images and captions, and prepare a presentation.

AV² by Weigl brings you media enhanced books that support active learning.

Try This!
Complete activities and hands-on experiments.

... and much, much more!

Published by AV² by Weigl
350 5th Avenue, 59th Floor
New York, NY 10118
Website: www.av2books.com   www.weigl.com

Library of Congress Cataloging-in-Publication Data

Craats, Rennay.
 New Mexico / Rennay Craats.
     p. cm. -- (A guide to American states)
 Includes index.
 ISBN 978-1-61690-803-4 (hardcover : alk. paper) -- ISBN 978-1-61690-479-1 (online)
 1. New Mexico--Juvenile literature. I. Title.
 F796.3.C733 2011
 978.9--dc23
                        2011019023

Printed in the United States of America in North Mankato, Minnesota

052011
WEP180511

Project Coordinator Jordan McGill
Art Director Terry Paulhus

Photo Credits
Every reasonable effort has been made to trace ownership and to obtain permission to reprint copyright material. The publishers would be pleased to have any errors or omissions brought to their attention so that they may be corrected in subsequent printings.

Weigl acknowledges Getty Images as its primary image supplier for this title.

Contents

Ship Rock, or Shiprock Peak, is the vent of an ancient volcano found in northwestern New Mexico. It is a National Natural Landmark and the subject of various American Indian legends.

Introduction

S cenic beauty and a rich cultural mix are two of the primary attractions in New Mexico. Nicknamed the Land of Enchantment, New Mexico has beautiful landscapes that enchant residents and visitors alike. The scenery varies from snowcapped mountains to scorching deserts. The state's culture is a fascinating blend of American Indian, Hispanic, and European influences, with ancient and modern ways mixed. New Mexico's Folk Arts Program helps preserve the traditional arts of these cultural groups. A program called the Arts Trails supports practicing artists, who take inspiration from the state's heritage and natural wonders.

Mild winds and temperatures make the Albuquerque International Balloon Fiesta possible each autumn. The New Mexico city is considered the ballooning capital of the world.

Early American Indians in New Mexico enlarged holes in cliffs and linked their rocky rooms to form clusters of cave dwellings.

The Pueblo Indians of northern New Mexico carry on traditions of their ancestors, who began farming in the region some 2,000 years ago. Along the Rio Grande, visitors can travel parts of El Camino Real, which means "The King's Highway." The roadway dates back to the late 1500s and was the first of its kind built by the Spanish in what is now the United States. Santa Fe, which means "Holy Faith" in Spanish, is one of the oldest U.S. towns. It was founded in 1610, a decade before the Pilgrims landed at Plymouth Rock. By contrast, some of the most sophisticated research facilities in the world are found in New Mexico. In 1945 the first atomic bomb was completed and tested in the state, after which scientists continued to conduct research in the fields of nuclear energy and space exploration.

Where Is New Mexico?

New Mexico is located in the southwestern United States. Almost square in shape, it shares borders with Colorado to the north and Oklahoma and Texas to the east. Texas also forms the state's southeast border. Arizona is to the west, and to the southwest New Mexico shares a border with the Mexican states of Chihuahua and Sonora. Along with Arizona, Utah, and Colorado, New Mexico forms what is known as the Four Corners, in which corners of all four states meet at one spot.

The Rio Grande, in the middle of the state, is one of the longest rivers in the United States. The Spanish began exploring the Rio Grande in the 1500s.

New Mexico is covered by thousands of miles of highways, including 25 scenic **byways**. Drivers heading north or south often use Interstate 25, and those driving east or west can take Interstate 40. Some travelers along Interstate 40 take the old byways that were part of Route 66. This was a historic roadway that started in Illinois, passed through New Mexico, and ended in California.

Air travel is made possible by international airports in Albuquerque and Roswell, a regional airport in Farmington, and various municipal and general aviation airports and runways. More than 6 million people pass through Albuquerque International Sunport every year.

The highest point in New Mexico is Wheeler Peak. It is 13,161 feet high.

New Mexico covers a land area of 121,356 square miles. It is the fifth-largest state in the country.

Spanish explorers of the 1560s named the area Nuevo Mexico, which is Spanish for "New Mexico." They hoped to discover riches similar to those found in Mexico. The name was changed to New Mexico when the area became part of the United States.

Since 1925 the official colors of New Mexico's flag have been red and yellow. These are the colors of Spain. On the flag, a sun of red rays appears in the center of a yellow background. The sun symbol is called a Zia. It is an ancient American Indian symbol that stands for the four directions and the four seasons. It stands for four parts of the day, from sunrise to noon to evening to night. It also stands for four parts of life, which are childhood, youth, middle age, and old age.

The famous railway called the Atchison, Topeka and Santa Fe is still operating, but as the Santa Fe Southern. It provides rides from Santa Fe to Lamy.

Mapping New Mexico

New Mexico has nearly 60,000 miles of highways. Interstates 10, 25, and 49 comprise approximately 1,000 miles of these roadways. The state's 26 Scenic Byways range from four to more than 600 miles long. A commuter rail line called the New Mexico Rail Runner runs north and south in the middle of the state.

Sites and Symbols

STATE SEAL
New Mexico

STATE BIRD
Roadrunner

STATE FLOWER
Yucca Flower

STATE FLAG
New Mexico

STATE ANIMAL
Black Bear

STATE TREE
Pinyon

Nickname The Land of Enchantment

Motto *Crescit Eundo* (It Grows as It Goes)

Song "O Fair New Mexico," words and music by Elizabeth Garret

Entered the Union January 6, 1912, as the 47th state

Capital Santa Fe

Population (2010 Census) 2,059,179 Ranked 36th state

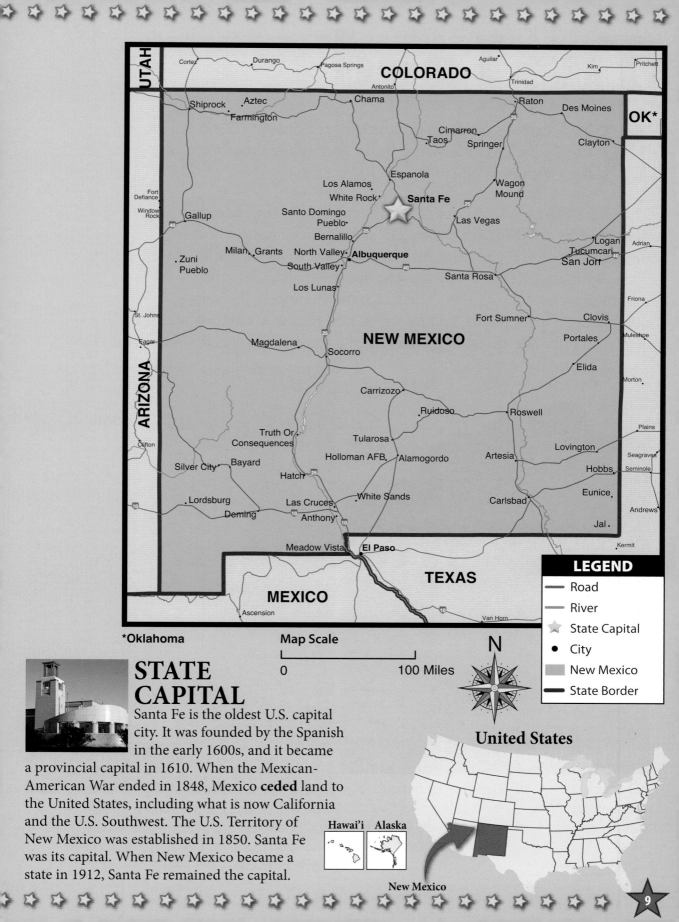

Map Labels

UTAH

COLORADO

Cortez • Durango • Pagosa Springs • Aguilar • Kim • Pritchett

Antonito • Trinidad

Shiprock • Aztec • Chama • Raton • Des Moines

Farmington • Cimarron • Springer • Clayton

Taos

OK*

Fort Defiance • Espanola • Wagon Mound

Los Alamos • **Santa Fe**

White Rock •

Window Rock • Santo Domingo Pueblo • Las Vegas

Gallup • Bernalillo

Milan • Grants • North Valley • **Albuquerque** • Logan • Adrian

Tucumcari • San Jon

• Zuni Pueblo • South Valley

Los Lunas • Santa Rosa

Friona

St. Johns • **NEW MEXICO**

Fort Sumner • Clovis

Eagar • Magdalena • Portales • Muleshoe

Socorro • Elida

Morton

Carrizozo

Plains

Clifton • Ruidoso • Roswell

Truth Or Consequences • Tularosa • Lovington • Seagraves

Silver City • Bayard • Holloman AFB • Alamogordo • Artesia • Seminole

Hatch • Hobbs

Eunice

Lordsburg • White Sands • Carlsbad • Andrews

Deming • Las Cruces

Anthony • Jal •

Kermit

Meadow Vista • El Paso

ARIZONA

MEXICO • **TEXAS**

Ascension • Van Horn

*Oklahoma

Map Scale

0 — 100 Miles

N

STATE CAPITAL

Santa Fe is the oldest U.S. capital city. It was founded by the Spanish in the early 1600s, and it became a provincial capital in 1610. When the Mexican-American War ended in 1848, Mexico **ceded** land to the United States, including what is now California and the U.S. Southwest. The U.S. Territory of New Mexico was established in 1850. Santa Fe was its capital. When New Mexico became a state in 1912, Santa Fe remained the capital.

United States

Hawai'i   Alaska

New Mexico

The Land

New Mexico is made up of four land regions: the Great Plains, the Rocky Mountains, the Basin and Range Province, and the Colorado Plateau.

The Great Plains, which cover the eastern third of the state, are **dissected** by canyons and rivers. The Rocky Mountains run along the north-central region around Santa Fe. Southwest of the Rockies is the Basin and Range Province. The southwest area features mountains and deep valleys. The Colorado Plateau in the state's northwest features plains, valleys, cliffs, and **mesas**. **Badlands** with dry lava plains are found in the southern part of the Colorado Plateau.

VALLEY OF FIRE

The rock formations in the Valley of Fire are ancient lava flows. Much of New Mexico's landscape was formed by volcanic activity, and various forms of volcanic rock are found in the state.

WHITE SANDS NATIONAL MONUMENT

The white sands of the White Sands National Monument cover 275 square miles. The sand dunes at the monument move from 5 to 40 feet per year.

RIO CHAMA

The Rio Chama was designated a Wild and Scenic River by the U.S. Congress. The Chama, Jemez, Puerco, Conchos, and Pecos rivers are all **tributaries** of the Rio Grande within New Mexico.

BOSQUE DEL APACHE

Bosque del Apache National Wildlife Refuge is popular with birdwatchers. Each winter tens of thousands of birds gather in the wetlands.

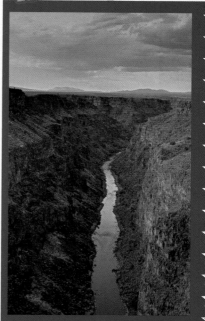

Though the Rio Grande is long, it is not very deep. The river's shallowness prevents it from being used as a shipping route.

Strong winds from the southwest move sand from one place to another at the White Sands National Monument. However, the main force causing the dunes to shift is gravity. Gravity pulls the sand downward. As it does, the leading edge, or slipface, of a dune grows ever steeper. As the sand is pulled down, the dune moves forward.

Hot springs rise up at many spots in the New Mexico landscape. The natural mineral waters are warmed by heat inside Earth.

The Albuquerque Convention and Visitors Bureau boasts that the city gets 310 days of sunshine annually.

Climate

N ew Mexico's climate is exceptionally sunny and dry throughout the year. The state's average annual temperature is around 64° Fahrenheit in the southeast and 40° F in the northern mountains. The temperature variation in the state is directly related to altitude. Temperatures fall by about 5° F with every 1,000-foot increase in elevation. In summer, areas at elevations below 5,000 feet quite often experience temperatures about 100° F. Even so, the low humidity and clear skies allow for rapid cooling at night.

The average annual precipitation in Santa Fe is roughly 14 inches per year. But averages can be misleading. There can be large differences in precipitation in New Mexico's desert and mountain regions.

Average Annual Precipitation Across New Mexico

The amount of rainfall recorded at different weather stations in New Mexico can vary widely. What features of New Mexico's geography do you think contribute to this variation?

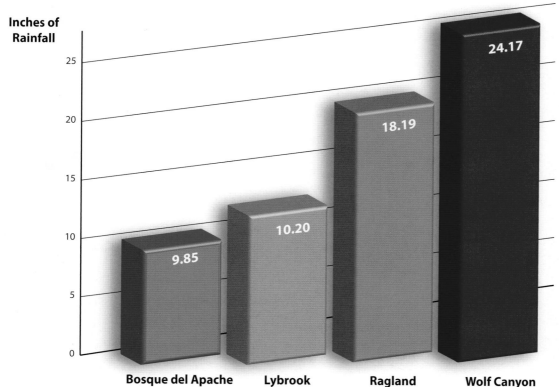

Inches of Rainfall

- Bosque del Apache: 9.85
- Lybrook: 10.20
- Ragland: 18.19
- Wolf Canyon: 24.17

Natural Resources

Natural gas, oil, and coal are among the state's valuable natural resources. The production of natural gas, oil, and coal employs thousands of people in the state. Most oil production occurs in southeastern New Mexico. Coal is found in northern New Mexico, most notably in the San Juan Basin and the Raton Basin. Most of the state's natural gas production also takes place in the San Juan Basin.

The New Mexico Energy, Minerals and Natural Resources Department regulates the oil wells in the state.

There are more than 15,000 abandoned mines in New Mexico. Active mines pay a fee that goes toward safeguarding or reclaiming the abandoned mines.

Copper is New Mexico's most valuable nonfuel mineral. The copper industry is located primarily in southwestern New Mexico. The state also has uranium reserves. Other important minerals produced in the state include perlite and potash. In addition, gold, molybdenum, and silver are mined.

The Rio Grande crosses the entire length of the state, flowing from north to south. Though the Rio Grande is not very deep, its water is used to **irrigate** crops along the river valley. Water is scarce in New Mexico. Most of New Mexico's lakes are actually **reservoirs**. The largest lake in the state is the Elephant Butte Reservoir, which was created by damming the Rio Grande.

New Mexico is the nation's leading producer of perlite, which is a natural glass in rock form that is created by the rapid cooling of lava.

In New Mexico, wetlands take up less than 1 percent of the state's land area. The wetland areas are especially important to birds that migrate to and through New Mexico.

The early mining towns were often plagued by fires and floods. Each time the buildings were destroyed, they were rebuilt with wood, stone, and adobe, a clay building material.

New Mexico was once called the Uranium Capital of the World. The state supplied the United States with most of its uranium needs after World War II. By the 1990s, however, uranium production slowed because of a decrease in demand.

The Navajo and Hopi operate coal mines and coal-fired power plants on a reservation spanning 17 million acres in Arizona, New Mexico, and Utah. New leadership, however, is turning to solar and wind power to meet the energy needs of these American Indians and their energy clients.

Plants

Gila National Forest, one of the largest national forests in the United States, covers 3.3 million acres in New Mexico. Apache-Sitgreaves, Carson, Cibola, Coronado, Lincoln, and Santa Fe national forests also beautify the state. Many wild plants, such as the creosote bush, the desert marigold, the desert zinnia, and the sunset cactus, grow in New Mexico.

The state's official flower, the yucca, grows in dry areas. The yucca looks like a pincushion of sharp leaves with a tall stalk growing out of it. In the spring, white flowers bloom from the end of the stalk. American Indians called the plant soapweed because the roots could be used to create hair tonic and soap. They also used yucca leaves to make rope, baskets, and even sandals. The pointed leaf tips were used as needles for sewing. The sharp leaves also earned the plant the nickname Spanish bayonet.

YUCCA

The yucca was selected by the state's schoolchildren as the state flower and officially adopted on March 14, 1927.

JUNIPER

Three-fourths of the state is covered by deep-green juniper shrubs, low pines, and prairie grasses. These plants grow well at elevations of about 4,000 feet to 7,000 feet.

POPPIES

Poppies dot the Florida Mountains with bright colors. *Florida* is Spanish for "feast of flowers."

PINYON PINE

The cones of pinyon pines produce large, edible pine nuts. The American Indians were the first people to harvest pine nuts in the region.

I DIDN'T KNOW THAT!

Several types of cactus found in the state's desert regions are endangered species, including the Knowlton cactus. A 12-acre area where this cactus still grows is under protection by the U.S. Fish and Wildlife Service.

There are nearly 40 threatened or endangered plants in New Mexico. They include the Mancos milkvetch, the southwestern prickly poppy, and Sneed's pincushion cactus.

The vegetation in each area of the state relates directly to the elevation in which it grows. From 8,500 to 9,500 feet above sea level, the dominant trees are blue spruce and Douglas fir.

A rootless water herb called the common bladderwort is the only native New Mexico plant known to trap and eat prey, such as tiny fish and insects.

Animals

Elk, deer, sheep, and porcupines live in forested parts of the state. The desert areas are home to jackrabbits, coyotes, and javelinas, which look like large boars. The Mexican wolf was once a common sight, but this type of wolf became endangered when its population dwindled to about 200. Fearing that the wolf would become extinct, conservationists worked to reestablish the animal in the wild. In 1998, they began to release wolves into federally protected areas of land, and many of these animals now roam in New Mexico's Gila National Forest.

Smaller and more abundant is the tarantula hawk wasp, the state's official insect. This metallic-blue wasp feeds on the nectar of flowers such as the milkweed, but it stalks more dangerous prey to feed its offspring. The wasp paralyzes tarantulas and uses the spiders as food for its developing **larvae**.

COYOTE

Coyotes roaming New Mexico's plains are able to move at speeds of 35 to 40 miles per hour. Their speed makes them powerful predators.

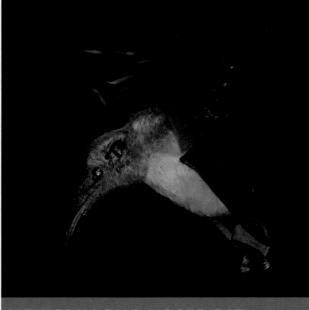

MEXICAN LONG-NOSED BAT

The Mexican long-nosed bat lives in New Mexico but is on the list of endangered animals in the United States. The bats eat only at night.

ROADRUNNER

The roadrunner, New Mexico's official bird, can run at speeds greater than 15 miles per hour. The roadrunner is also known by its Spanish name, *el correcaminos*. Its diet consists of insects, lizards, and snakes.

JAVELINA

The javelina is also known as the collared peccary. It is the only pig-like animal that is native to the United States and found in the wild. The javelina has poor eyesight but excellent hearing.

I DIDN'T KNOW THAT!

The Loach minnow and the southwestern willow flycatcher live in the Gila Riparian Preserve, located in Grant County. The preserve protects the Gila River and its surroundings. It safeguards animal species that are considered threatened or endangered.

Black bears are not always black. In New Mexico, some black bears are the color of cinnamon. Others are quite blonde.

Carlsbad Caverns National Park has a summer colony of hundreds of thousands of Mexican free-tailed bats living in what is known as the Bat Cave. Each evening at sunset they swarm out of the cave's entrance to feed in the surrounding area.

Tourism

Millions of people a year travel to New Mexico to experience its many recreational, historical, and geographical wonders. Santa Fe is the primary destination for visitors. It is located in the beautiful Sangre de Cristo Mountains and known for Spanish and American Indian art. Many galleries can be found along Canyon Road, its main street. The city also has the Georgia O'Keeffe Museum, which displays paintings created by O'Keeffe, a famous artist who lived and worked in New Mexico for many years.

The supernatural also draws tourists. Some people believe that Roswell, in the southeast, was the site of an alien spacecraft crash in 1947. Today the city is the location of the International UFO Museum and Research Center.

SANTA FE

The Plaza in Santa Fe attracts shoppers as well as museum and restaurant–goers. American Indians sell crafts at the Palace of the Governors.

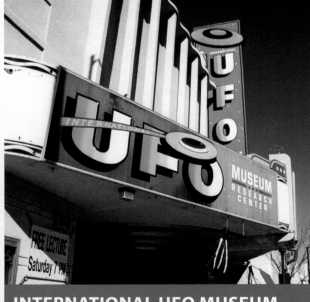

INTERNATIONAL UFO MUSEUM

The International UFO Museum and Research Center is devoted to **phenomena** concerning unidentified flying object, or UFO, sightings and landings in the United States. It is an international center for UFO information, with a research library containing more than 3,000 books on the subject.

CARLSBAD CAVERNS

Carlsbad Caverns National Park contains more than 100 limestone caves, many of which tourists can explore.

MUSEUM OF SPACE HISTORY

The New Mexico Museum of Space History is located in Alamogordo. In addition to the space exhibits, the site features the International Space Hall of Fame.

I DIDN'T KNOW THAT!

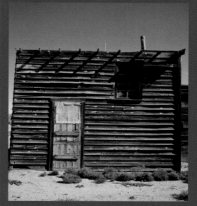

New Mexico has over 400 ghost towns. There are few buildings left in the ghost towns. But these sites still tell the state's history. Among the best-known are Cabezon, Mogollon, and White Oaks.

Billy the Kid was born William H. Bonney, Jr., in New York City. He moved to New Mexico with his mother while in his early teens. He soon became a thief and gunfighter. Billy the Kid was said to have killed at least 27 men, including two deputies. In 1881, Sheriff Pat Garrett shot and killed Billy the Kid at Fort Sumner. Visitors to Fort Sumner can see the Billy the Kid Museum.

The War Eagles Museum in Santa Teresa displays fighter planes from World War II, jet-fighter aircraft from the Korean War, and antique cars.

Industry

Now Mexicans work in printing and publishing, electronics, and stone and glass production. As in other states, service industries such as health care employ the most people. The state is renowned, however, for high-technology industries. One important high-technology facility is Sandia National Laboratories. Owned by the federal government, Sandia has operated in Albuquerque since the late 1940s. Over the years, this company has developed and tested rockets and weapons as well as conducted safety research for the nuclear energy industry.

Industries in New Mexico
Value of Goods and Services in Millions of Dollars

Several major industries are grouped together in some economic categories. But mining alone accounts for 7 percent of the state's economy, which is higher than in most other states. Why is mining especially important to New Mexico's people and economy?

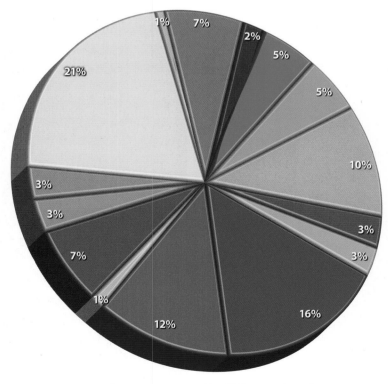

Percentages may not add to 100 because of rounding.

LEGEND

Agriculture, Forestry, and Fishing	$1,088
Mining	$5,022
Utilities	$1,469
Construction	$3,861
Manufacturing	$3,963
Wholesale and Retail Trade	$7,593
Transportation	$1,917
Media and Entertainment	$2,669
Finance, Insurance, and Real Estate	$11,929
Professional and Technical Services	$9,151
Education	$454
Health Care	$5,580
Hotels and Restaurants	$2,557
Other Services	$2,126
Government	$15,423
TOTAL	**$74,802**

About 50 miles west of Socorro are 27 enormous, dish-shaped antennae known as the Very Large Array, or VLA. The **antennae** form a type of telescope that receives radio waves from distant galaxies. The information received by each of the dishes is combined to create a more complete view of the universe. Each antenna is 82 feet wide and weighs 230 tons.

Rockets are tested at the White Sands Missile Range, which is located on the same land where the first atomic bomb was tested.

Goods and Services

Manufacturing, mining, construction, and agriculture are four traditional industries that account for close to one-fifth of New Mexico's economy. The rest of its economy is made up of the service sector. Trade, banking, insurance, and real estate are the biggest moneymaking services. Goods and services provided by federal, state, and local governments account for more than $15 billion of New Mexico's annual economy.

Although not as important to the state's economy as it once was, agriculture employs about 24,500 New Mexicans. Another 84,000 residents work in food processing. Meat from beef cattle and milk provided by dairy cows are top agricultural products. Eggs and poultry are also important. Hay, pecans, onions, and chili peppers are the state's leading crops. Farmers also raise greenhouse and nursery items, such as trees for landscaping.

New Mexico is a leading producer of chili peppers. Thousands of different varieties of hot peppers are grown in the state.

The state is known for computer technology. Intel, one of the world's largest manufacturers of computer chips, built its first fully automated manufacturing plant in Rio Rancho. Among its many products, the company created a large memory chip that does not need to be refreshed periodically.

Albuquerque is New Mexico's major manufacturing center. Food and beverage manufacturers, such as cereal and tortilla makers, have been growing in the past decade. Furniture companies, such as mattress maker Tempur-Pedic, have relocated to the state. Electronics producers remain, however, the largest manufacturing employers in the state. Producers of semiconductors and silicon and other wafers used in computers do business in New Mexico, as do producers of electronics parts. Honeywell International manufactures military communication systems and other products.

Space products are also a valuable part of the goods-producing sector. The government funds several top research laboratories, as well as military bases, throughout the state.

American Indians

The state's early inhabitants arrived in the region more than 12,000 years ago. **Archaeologists** have found stone spearheads that indicate that the prehistoric people of New Mexico hunted mammoths and bison. The Cochise were among the first American Indian cultures that developed in the desert areas of western New Mexico. The group existed between 9,000 and 2,000 years ago. For food, the Cochise gathered edible plants and hunted. During the later stages of the culture's progress, the people grew plants for harvesting.

About 2,200 years ago, the hunter-gatherers of the Mogollon culture settled in the southwestern part of New Mexico. They lived in small villages and probably raised plants for food. The Mogollon were the first people to make pottery in the Southwest.

At Chaco Culture National Historical Park, visitors can see the foundations of buildings constructed by the Chacoan people. They flourished in the area from 850 to 1250.

The Navajo are the largest American Indian group in the United States. They call themselves the Dineh or the Dine. They call their homeland Dinetah.

The ancient 70-acre Acoma Pueblo, known as Sky City, is thought to be the oldest continuously inhabited city in the United States.

In 1864 thousands of Navajo were forced to make the long and dangerous journey to Bosque Redondo Reservation. This trip is known as the Long Walk.

Ancient stone spearheads, called points, have been found at sites near the cities of Clovis and Folsom. The spearheads are described as either Clovis or Folsom based on differences in shape. Folsom points tend to be shorter. Clovis points are generally thicker.

Trails overlook the Tyuonyi ruins at Bandelier National Monument. The outlines of a circular settlement, or pueblo, can be seen quite clearly from above. The monument features many 13th century ruins and remains.

Another hunter-gatherer group, the Ancestral Puebloans, sometimes called the Anasazi, lived in northwestern New Mexico. They built multistoried cliff dwellings but abandoned them in the late 1200s, probably because of a severe drought. The Pueblo Indians of modern New Mexico are their descendants. The word *pueblo* is Spanish for "village" or "town." The Pueblo groups include the Zuni, the Acoma, and the Laguna.

During the 1400s the Navajo and the Apache settled in what is now New Mexico. The Navajo settled west of the Pueblo. The Apache spread out over eastern and southern New Mexico.

Explorers and Missionaries

The first Europeans to visit New Mexico were Spaniards searching for cities of gold. After being shipwrecked off the Texas coast in 1528, the Spaniard Álvar Núñez Cabeza de Vaca and three other survivors spent the next eight years wandering through what is now the southwestern United States and northern Mexico. During their journey they encountered American Indians who told them about a kingdom of riches located farther north. Upon his return to Europe, Núñez wrote about his shipwreck and the stories he had heard about the kingdom, which came to be known as the Seven Golden Cities of Cíbola.

After the Núñez story became known, Spanish leaders planned an **expedition** to find the Golden Cities. A priest named Marcos de Niza was sent in advance, with a guide named Estéban. The guide was a survivor of the Núñez group. In 1539, the scouts entered what is now New Mexico. The priest saw a large Zuni settlement from the distance and returned with exaggerated tales of its grandeur. In 1540 the explorer Francisco Vázquez de Coronado traveled to the area to find the promised riches, and he found nothing but the mud buildings of the Zuni Pueblo.

Francisco Vázquez de Coronado led an expedition to conquer the Seven Golden Cities of Cíbola. In literature, the cities are also known as El Dorado. Though El Dorado was never found, the group did discover the Grand Canyon.

Timeline of Settlement

Early Exploration

1536 Spaniard Álvar Núñez Cabeza de Vaca and companions are rescued after wandering the region following a shipwreck. They begin spreading rumors they heard from the American Indians, about a kingdom of riches called the Seven Golden Cities.

1539 Marcos de Niza, a priest, and his guide Estéban reach what is now New Mexico. They had been sent to scout the location of the Seven Cities.

1540 The Spanish explorer Francisco Vázquez de Coronado leads an expedition to the area.

1563 Francisco de Ibarra, another Spaniard, arrives, looking for gold.

First Settlements

1598 Juan de Oñate founds the first European settlement, recorded in rock inscriptions, and is named the governor of the Province of New Mexico.

1608 At about this time, Santa Fe is established. In 1610, it is named the provincial capital.

1680 The Pueblo Indians begin a major uprising against the Spanish. The Spanish work to retake control of the area for more than a decade.

Changes of Control

1821 After the Mexican War of Independence, the Province of New Mexico becomes part of Mexico.

1848 Following the Mexican-American War, the land that is now New Mexico becomes part of the United States.

Territory and Statehood

1850 The New Mexico Territory is established. It includes most of what is now Arizona. In 1863, the territory is divided, and the Territory of Arizona is created.

1912 The U.S. Congress passes a measure to admit New Mexico to the Union. President William Howard Taft makes New Mexico's statehood official.

Early Settlers

I n 1598 Juan de Oñate led 400 Spanish settlers north from what is now Mexico, then called New Spain. They ended up in northern New Mexico at San Gabriel, where the Rio Grande and Chama rivers meet. The Acoma Pueblo revolted against the newcomers in late 1598. In retaliation, the Spanish killed hundreds of the Acoma.

Map of Settlements and Resources in Early New Mexico

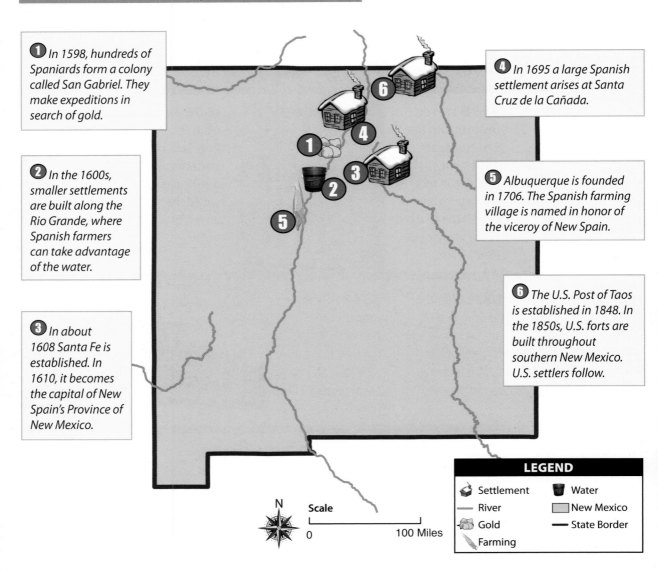

1 In 1598, hundreds of Spaniards form a colony called San Gabriel. They make expeditions in search of gold.

2 In the 1600s, smaller settlements are built along the Rio Grande, where Spanish farmers can take advantage of the water.

3 In about 1608 Santa Fe is established. In 1610, it becomes the capital of New Spain's Province of New Mexico.

4 In 1695 a large Spanish settlement arises at Santa Cruz de la Cañada.

5 Albuquerque is founded in 1706. The Spanish farming village is named in honor of the viceroy of New Spain.

6 The U.S. Post of Taos is established in 1848. In the 1850s, U.S. forts are built throughout southern New Mexico. U.S. settlers follow.

N

Scale

0   100 Miles

LEGEND

Settlement		Water	
River		New Mexico	
Gold		State Border	
Farming			

Unrest continued, and the Pueblo burned Santa Fe in 1680. The Spanish did not reestablish their authority in the area until more than a decade later.

Santa Fe became the center of Spanish settlement in the north, and Albuquerque was the population center in the south. As the 1800s began, New Mexico had more people than Texas and California, and all three areas were controlled by Spain. In 1821, Mexico won its independence from Spain, and these lands came under Mexican rule. That same year Captain William Becknell of the United States opened the Santa Fe Trail to transport goods between Missouri and New Mexico.

In 1846, war began between the United States and Mexico. Under the Treaty of Guadalupe Hidalgo ending the war in 1848, New Mexico became part of the United States. In 1850 the U.S. government established the New Mexico Territory. As the territory grew, it began to attract the cowboys, miners, railroad workers, gamblers, and cattle **rustlers** who settled this new U.S. frontier.

The adobe church of San Felipe de Neri, in Albuquerque, was built in 1793.

I DIDN'T KNOW THAT!

The Santa Fe Trail was an important trade route for goods and people until the railroad took its place in 1880.

At his ranch near Roswell, John Chisum developed the largest cattle herd in the United States during the second half of the 1800s.

The leader of the Pueblo Revolt of 1680 was Popé, a Tewa Pueblo medicine man. After driving the Spanish from Santa Fe, Popé tried to wipe out all elements of Spanish culture and the Christian religion. In 1692 the Spanish governor Diego de Vargas reclaimed the area. Colonists and priests returned to New Mexico and built homes and missions in and around Santa Fe.

Zebulon Pike led a U.S. Army expedition into New Mexico in 1806. His report of the trip brought greater numbers of American trappers and traders into the area.

The first territorial governor of the U.S. Territory of New Mexico was James C. Calhoun.

New Mexico became the 47th state on January 6, 1912. The new state's population was approximately 327,000.

Notable People

New Mexico is the birthplace or adopted home of many U.S. business leaders, such as Conrad Hilton, who established the Hilton Hotels chain, and Jeff Bezos, founder of Amazon.com. New Mexicans have served as scientists and military leaders. They have governed the state and helped lead the nation, politically and intellectually.

DENNIS CHAVEZ
(1888–1962)

Dennis Chavez was honored by the U.S. Postal Service as part of the Great American stamp series. Born in Los Chaves, in what was then the New Mexico Territory, he had to quit school in eighth grade to help support his family. Over time, however, he earned a law degree. A Democrat, he began serving in the state legislature in 1923. From 1931 to 1935, he served in the U.S. House of Representatives. In 1936 he became the first Hispanic American elected to the U.S. Senate, where he served until his death.

CLINTON PRESBA ANDERSON
(1895–1975)

Clinton Presba Anderson moved to New Mexico when he became seriously ill with tuberculosis. After he recovered, he became a journalist. He reported on the state legislature. Later, he entered the insurance business. Anderson's first political position was as New Mexico's state treasurer. He later served in the U.S. House of Representatives, as secretary of agriculture, and in the U.S. Senate.

JOSEPH MANUEL MONTOYA (1915–1978)

When elected to the New Mexico House of Representatives in 1936, Joseph Montoya was 21 years old, the youngest person to ever have won that office. In 1940, when Montoya began service as a state senator, he was the youngest to serve in the state senate. Montoya was the lieutenant governor of New Mexico from 1947 to 1957. He then went to Washington, D.C., serving in both the U.S. House of Representatives and in the U.S. Senate.

PETE DOMENICI (1932–)

Pete Domenici was a U.S. senator from New Mexico from 1973 to 2009, the longest service of any senator in the state's history. A Republican, Domenici was an advocate for nuclear power. He also worked to try to achieve insurance coverage for the cost of mental health services.

SID GUTIERREZ (1951–)

Born in Albuquerque, Sid Gutierrez was the first Hispanic American to both pilot and command a U.S. space shuttle. Before joining NASA, he served in the U.S. Air Force, logging more than 4,500 hours of flight time. He was inducted into the International Space Hall of Fame in 1995.

I DIDN'T KNOW THAT!

Lew Wallace (1827–1905) was born before the state existed. He was appointed the governor of the New Mexico Territory in 1878. While governor, he wrote the novel *Ben-Hur: A Tale of Christ*. It became the best-selling U.S. novel of the 19th century.

Bill Richardson (1947–) moved his young family to New Mexico in 1978. He was elected to the U.S. House of Representatives for seven consecutive terms. During his eighth term, President Bill Clinton asked him to serve as the U.S. ambassador to the U.N. After that, Richardson was the U.S. secretary of energy. In 2002, he was elected governor of New Mexico, a post he held until 2011.

Population

ew Mexico ranks 36th among the states in total population. At the time of the 2010 Census it had about 2 million residents, with most living in urban areas. Because of its historical ties and **proximity** to Mexico, about 46 percent of New Mexicans claim Hispanic origins. This is much higher than the same figure for the country's population as a whole. The United States population is approximately 16 percent Hispanic American. About 10 percent of the New Mexico's population is American Indian, much higher than the national figure of about 1 percent. Many American Indians live on reservations in the central and northwestern parts of the state.

New Mexico Population 1950–2010

In this time frame, the state's rate of population growth has been above the national average. What are some of the factors that have helped New Mexico grow more rapidly than many other states?

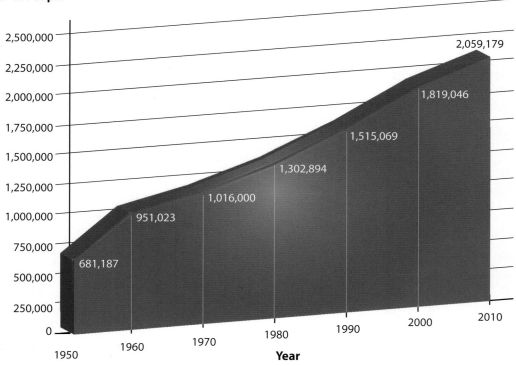

Number of People

2,059,179

1,819,046

1,515,069

1,302,894

1,016,000

951,023

681,187

2,500,000
2,250,000
2,000,000
1,750,000
1,500,000
1,250,000
1,000,000
750,000
500,000
250,000
0

1950   1960   1970   1980   1990   2000   2010

Year

New Mexico has 22 American Indian groups, including more than one-third of the nation's Navajo people.

The University of New Mexico, in Albuquerque, is the state's largest university, with more than 32,000 students.

The Albuquerque metropolitan area experienced rapid population growth in the late 20th and early 21st centuries. The metropolitan area is on track to have a million inhabitants by 2016.

The most populous city in New Mexico is Albuquerque. Other large cities include Las Cruces, Rio Rancho, Santa Fe, and Roswell.

New Mexico has a small population in relation to its large size. There are only about 17 people per square mile of land. The national average is more than 87 people per square mile.

Population growth around Albuquerque has been especially dramatic east of the Tijeras Canyon. For a long time, the canyon served as an obstacle to growth, but bridges and roads have since been built. People in the area now refer to the canyon as the I-40 Canyon, because Interstate 40 runs across it.

Humble City was once the smallest town with a radio station, but it lost its radio license in 2011 after it was determined that the town had a population of zero.

Politics and Government

New Mexico's constitution has been in place since 1911, although it has been amended many times since then. Amendments and bills are proposed by either the Senate or the House of Representatives in the state's legislative branch of government, which meets in the **capitol**. If a bill is approved by a majority of the 42 senators and 70 representatives, it is sent to the governor to make into law. If the governor **vetoes** the bill, the legislative branch can still pass it if enough members vote for it again.

New Mexico's capitol, located in Santa Fe, is one of the newest state capitols in the United States. It was opened in 1966. It is the only round capitol in the nation.

When New Mexico was a territory, construction was started on a capitol, but the funds ran out and the Civil War drew attention elsewhere. In 1889, the "state house" was completed. It was used as a territorial courthouse and now serves as a federal courthouse.

The governor heads the executive branch of the government. This branch develops policies and plans for the state's future. The governor also appoints many important state officials.

The judicial branch of New Mexico's government ensures that the state's laws are followed. It consists of several types of courts. The highest court in New Mexico is the Supreme Court. The next highest court is the Court of Appeals, and there are 13 district courts, 54 magistrate courts, and various lower courts.

Cultural Groups

Most Hispanic Americans who live in the state speak Spanish. There are many Spanish-language newspapers and TV and radio programs. Hispanic Americans celebrate their culture in New Mexico with a variety of festivals and events. The Spanish Market, for example, gives Hispanic American craftspeople a chance to showcase their art. It is held in Santa Fe twice yearly, in summer and winter. Each September the Santa Fe Fiesta celebrates Hispanic American culture with dances, concerts, and parades.

New Mexico has 19 Pueblo Indian villages. Taos Pueblo is a National Historic Landmark and a World Heritage Site. Zuni Pueblo is the state's largest and most populous Pueblo site.

Some of the ceremonies and festivals held in the pueblos are longstanding traditions. Zuni Pueblo holds the Shalako ceremony in winter. During the ceremony people dressed as **kachinas** enter the village and perform **rituals** to bring rain, a bountiful harvest, and good fortune in the coming year. Pueblo feast days are celebrated throughout the state. San Geronimo Feast Day at Taos Pueblo features traditional dancing as well as a trade fair displaying drums, pottery, and clothing.

The Navajo and the Pueblo Indians have a unique tradition of painting with sand. Used in healing ceremonies, the fragile pictures depict animals, plants, and other important symbols.

Each village has its own pottery style. For many American Indians, pottery is an important part of their culture. Some use pottery in birth ceremonies and as part of funeral ceremonies.

Many of the state's American Indians celebrate their culture with festivals and ceremonies. Navajo craft traditions, such as the making of turquoise jewelry and woven rugs, have been passed down from generation to generation. Every August, Gallup hosts the Inter-Tribal Indian Ceremonial. This popular event features powwows, rodeo events, arts, and a parade.

Candlelit paper bags are common decorations in New Mexico during the December holidays. Streets are lined with these glowing paper bags. They are known as farolitos or luminarias.

Mexican food is popular throughout New Mexico. The people of Las Cruces celebrate the cuisine in an annual fall festival called the Whole Enchilada Fiesta. The events include the making of the "Whole Enchilada," reputed to be the world's largest. The cooks use 250 pounds of corn dough to make a monster tortilla. The tortilla is carried by 14 people to specially made equipment that is big enough to fry it.

The Pueblo Indians associate turquoise with the sky. Turquoise was traditionally used as a ritual offering or trade item.

The first Spanish language newspaper in the state was *El Crepusculo de la Libertad*, which means "The Dawn of Liberty." It was first printed in 1834 in Santa Fe.

At Gran Quivira visitors can see the remains of ancient stone houses that Pueblo Indians lived in until the end of the 17th century. The remains of several kivas are also there to view. Kivas were underground structures used for ceremonial meetings.

Arts and Entertainment

New Mexico's unique landscape and culture have long influenced writers and artists. In the 1920s the acclaimed English novelist D. H. Lawrence lived outside Taos, writing *The Plumed Serpent*. Perhaps the most noted U.S. author associated with New Mexico is Willa Cather. Her 1927 novel *Death Comes to the Archbishop* is a study of Roman Catholic missionaries in New Mexico. The author Tony Hillerman lived in New Mexico as a young man. His mystery novels, such as *A Thief of Time*, explore Navajo traditions.

The town of Taos attracts artists and craftspeople, and many of its buildings reflect artistic spirit. Famous artists who have stayed in Taos include the painter Marsden Hartley and the photographers Alfred Stieglitz and Ansel Adams.

Among visual artists, perhaps the most famous associated with the state is Georgia O'Keeffe. She painted objects such as flowers and animal skulls in an **abstract** way. She also painted scenes of the New Mexican landscape. The black-on-black pottery made by Santa Fe artist Maria Martinez in the early 1900s is now prized by collectors and art museums. The black-and-white photography of Ansel Adams has been popularized on posters and calendars.

While enjoying the Santa Fe Opera, audiences at the opera company's outdoor theater take in breathtaking views of the foothills of the Sangre de Cristo Mountains. Albuquerque's New Mexico Symphony Orchestra and groups in other cities perform classical concerts.

Both the Santa Fe Playhouse and the Albuquerque Little Theater have been staging performances since the early 1900s. Actor Freddie Prinze, Jr., grew up in Albuquerque. Actress Demi Moore was born in Roswell. She moved from soap operas to films such as *St. Elmo's Fire* and *Ghost*.

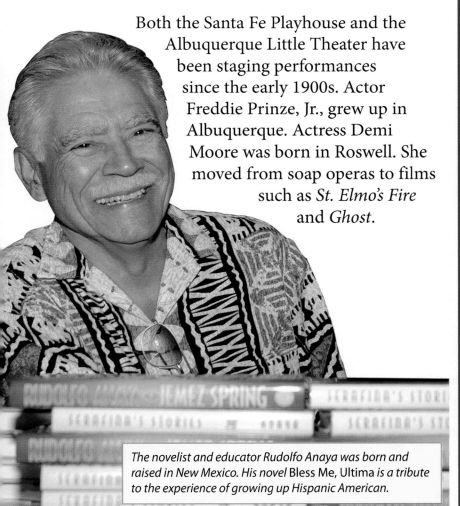

The novelist and educator Rudolfo Anaya was born and raised in New Mexico. His novel Bless Me, Ultima *is a tribute to the experience of growing up Hispanic American.*

Sports

Albuquerque hosts a hot-air balloon festival every fall. The Albuquerque International Balloon Fiesta attracts large crowds who watch hundreds of balloons floating overhead. This event is not a race, but participants do compete. Prizes are given to the balloonist who can best perform certain feats, such as landing closest to a specified spot.

Skiing is a favorite winter sport in New Mexico. Angel Fire is a top ski resort located north of Santa Fe in the Sangre de Cristo Mountains. In the winter, snowboarders and skiers are challenged to conquer the slopes or explore the trails on cross-country skis. Angel Fire offers skiing runs for beginning and advanced skiers. In the summer the trails are open to mountain biking, hiking, and horseback riding. There is also a golf course in this beautiful mountain area.

Taos Ski Valley has 110 trails. About half the trails are "expert" level. About one-quarter of the trails are for "beginners." The rest are "intermediate."

For safety's sake, the number of balloons at the Albuquerque International Balloon Fiesta has been capped at 750.

Though New Mexico does not have teams in the major professional sports leagues, it has been home to some great professional athletes. Pittsburgh Pirates outfielder Ralph Kiner was one of the greatest sluggers in the team's history. During each of his first seven years as a Pirate, Kiner led the National League in home runs. In 1949 he had 127 runs batted-in, which was best in the league that year. His contribution to the game was officially recognized in 1975, when he was inducted into the Baseball Hall of Fame.

The Unser family, from Albuquerque, has dominated auto racing for decades. Brothers Bobby and Al Unser were racers during the 1960s, 1970s, and 1980s. Bobby won the Indianapolis 500 race three times, and Al won it four times. Al's fourth win took place in 1987, when he was 48 years old. His son, Al Unser, Jr., won the Indianapolis 500 twice in the 1990s. Now, Jason Unser and Al Unser III are vying for titles.

National Averages Comparison

T he United States is a federal republic, consisting of fifty states and the District of Columbia. Alaska and Hawai'i are the only non-contiguous, or non-touching, states in the nation. Today, the United States of America is the third-largest country in the world in population. The United States Census Bureau takes a census, or count of all the people, every ten years. It also regularly collects other kinds of data about the population and the economy. How does New Mexico compare to the national average?

Comparison Chart

United States 2010 Census Data *	USA	New Mexico
Admission to Union	NA	January 6, 1912
Land Area (in square miles)	3,537,438.44	121,355.53
Population Total	308,745,538	2,059,179
Population Density (people per square mile)	87.28	16.97
Population Percentage Change (April 1, 2000, to April 1, 2010)	9.7%	13.2%
White Persons (percent)	72.4%	68.4%
Black Persons (percent)	12.6%	2.1%
American Indian and Alaska Native Persons (percent)	0.9%	9.4%
Asian Persons (percent)	4.8%	1.4%
Native Hawaiian and Other Pacific Islander Persons (percent)	0.2%	0.1%
Some Other Race (percent)	6.2%	15.0%
Persons Reporting Two or More Races (percent)	2.9%	3.7%
Persons of Hispanic or Latino Origin (percent)	16.3%	46.3%
Not of Hispanic or Latino Origin (percent)	83.7%	53.7%
Median Household Income	$52,029	$43,719
Percentage of People Age 25 or Over Who Have Graduated from High School	80.4%	78.9%

*All figures are based on the 2010 United States Census, with the exception of the last two items. Percentages may not add to 100 because of rounding.

How to Improve My Community

S trong communities make strong states. Think about what features are important in your community. What do you value? Education? Health? Forests? Safety? Beautiful spaces? Government works to help citizens create ideal living conditions that are fair to all by providing services in communities. Consider what changes you could make in your community. How would they improve your state as a whole? Using this concept web as a guide, write a report that outlines the features you think are most important in your community and what improvements could be made. A strong state needs strong communities.

What features make excellent communities and states? Consider features such as education, jobs, and social services. In an ideal state, what features do you think are most essential?

In what ways does your state meet your standards for an ideal state? What services does it provide your community?

In what ways could your state be improved to bring its living conditions closer to those of an ideal state? What services should be provided in your community?

**2.
Your State**

**1.
Ideal State**

**3.
Potential
Improvements**

**How
Would You
Improve Your
State?**

**4.
Obstacles**

**5.
Solutions**

What are some solutions to the obstacles that you found?

What are some obstacles that could prevent the changes you outlined from being instituted?

Exercise Your Mind!

Think about these questions and then use your research skills to find the answers and learn more fascinating facts about New Mexico. A teacher, librarian, or parent may be able to help you locate the best sources to use in your research.

1. What was the lure of the Seven Golden Cities of Cíbola?

2. Who was Pancho Villa?

3. What is the "Roswell incident"?

4. What did J. Robert Oppenheimer do in New Mexico?

5. What was the Long Walk?

6. Who were Chiefs Victorio and Geronimo?

7. What is unique about the Tucumcari Historical Research Institute and Museum?

8. What is El Camino Real?

Words to Know

abstract: creative artwork that may not represent an object realistically

antennae: metal rods or wire devices by which radio waves are sent and received

archaeologists: scientists who study early peoples through their artifacts and remains

badlands: dry places where rapid erosion has cut strange shapes in the soil or rocks

byways: side roads

capitol: the building for the legislature

ceded: transferred land by treaty

dissected: separated or divided

expedition: a journey for a specific purpose

irrigate: to transport water to farmland

kachinas: among the Pueblo Indians, ancestral spirits that visit the living

larvae: insect offspring in a wormlike stage

mesas: high plateaus with steep sides

phenomena: events that are considered unusual or extraordinary

proximity: nearness

reservoirs: storage areas created to collect and store water for future use

rituals: series of actions used in a religious ceremony

rustlers: cattle thieves

tributaries: rivers or streams that join a larger river

vetoes: uses political authority to reject a proposed bill or law

Index

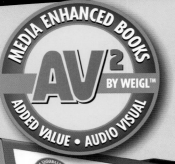

Log on to www.av2books.com

AV² by Weigl brings you media enhanced books that support active learning. Go to www.av2books.com, and enter the special code found on page 2 of this book. You will gain access to enriched and enhanced content that supplements and complements this book. Content includes video, audio, web links, quizzes, a slide show, and activities.

Audio
Listen to sections of the book read aloud.

Video
Watch informative video clips.

Embedded Weblinks
Gain additional information for research.

Try This!
Complete activities and hands-on experiments.

WHAT'S ONLINE?

Try This!	Embedded Weblinks	Video	EXTRA FEATURES
Test your knowledge of the state in a mapping activity.	Discover more attractions in New Mexico.	Watch a video introduction to New Mexico.	**Audio** Listen to sections of the book read aloud.
Find out more about precipitation in your city.	Learn more about the history of the state.	Watch a video about the features of the state.	
Plan what attractions you would like to visit in the state.	Learn the full lyrics of the state song.		**Key Words** Study vocabulary, and complete a matching word activity.
Learn more about the early natural resources of the state.			
Write a biography about a notable resident of New Mexico.			**Slide Show** View images and captions, and prepare a presentation
Complete an educational census activity.			**Quizzes** Test your knowledge.

AV² was built to bridge the gap between print and digital. We encourage you to tell us what you like and what you want to see in the future.

Sign up to be an AV² Ambassador at www.av2books.com/ambassador.